ANIMAL ABILITIES

OCTOPUSES

Anna Claybourne

Raintree is an imprint of Capstone Global Library Limited, a company incorporated in England and Wales having its registered office at 7 Pilgrim Street, London, EC4V 6LB – Registered company number: 6695582

To contact Raintree, please phone 0845 6044371, fax + 44 (0) 1865 312263, or email myorders@ raintreepublishers.co.uk.

Edited by Laura Knowles, Abby Colich, and Diyan Leake
Designed by Victoria Allen
Original illustrations © Capstone Global Library Ltd 2013
Illustrated by HL Studios
Picture research by Elizabeth Alexander
Originated by Capstone Global Library Ltd
Printed and bound in China by CTPS

ISBN 978 1 406 25912 4
17 16 15 14 13
10 9 8 7 6 5 4 3 2 1

British Library Cataloguing in Publication Data
Claybourne, Anna.
   Octopuses. -- (Animal abilities)
   1. Octopuses--Juvenile literature. 2. Animal intelligence--Juvenile literature.
   I. Title II. Series
   594.5'6-dc23

Acknowledgements
We would like to thank the following for permission to reproduce photographs: Alamy p. 25 (© Jeff Rotman); Corbis pp. 14 (© Stringer/ New Zealand/X01244/Reuters), 22 (© Bettmann), 28 (© Will Gray/JAI), 29 (© Melvin G. Tarpley/ US Army/Handout/Reuters); © Kaylene Kau www.coroflot.com/kaylene p. 26; The Maritime Aquarium at Norwalk (CT, USA) p. 21; Nature Picture Library pp. 7 (© David Shale), 8 (© Jeff Rotman), 9 (© Jeff Rotman), 12 (© Jose B. Ruiz), 15 (© Nature Production), 17 (© Constantinos Petrinos); Photoshot pp. 13 (David Fleetham), 20 (Picture Alliance/Jens Büttner); Shutterstock pp. 4 (© Rich Carey), 6 (© Bjorn Stefanson), 11 (© Mike Bauer), 18 (© EcoPrint), 23 (© bluehand), 24 (© Boris Pamikov); Superstock p. 19 (© Masa Ushioda/age footstock); Tamar Gutnick p. 16; Visuals Unlimited, Inc. p. 27 (Massimo Brega/ The Lighthouse). Design feature of an octopus silhoutte reproduced with permission of Shutterstock (© Potapov Alexander).

Cover photograph of a coconut shell octopus reproduced with permission of Corbis (© Hal Beral).

Every effort has been made to contact copyright holders of material reproduced in this book. Any omissions will be rectified in subsequent printings if notice is given to the publisher.

Contents

Meet the octopus 4

Being an octopus 6

Octopus bodies 8

Octopus brains and senses 10

In disguise 12

Learning 14

Solving problems 16

Sneaky tricks 18

Having fun 20

Humans and octopuses 22

Octopus science 24

Copying the octopus 26

The amazing octopus 28

Glossary 30

Find out more 31

Index 32

Some words are shown in bold, **like this**. You can find out what they mean by looking in the glossary.

Meet the octopus

Even if you've never met an octopus, you'll know one when you see one! There's nothing else quite like this slippery sea creature.

Arms or legs?

The word *octopus* means "eight feet" – but octopuses don't have feet! They have eight long, slithery arms that can crawl, stretch, and curl around objects. The arms are often called legs or **tentacles**. However, true tentacles, which **squid** have, are longer and thinner than octopus arms.

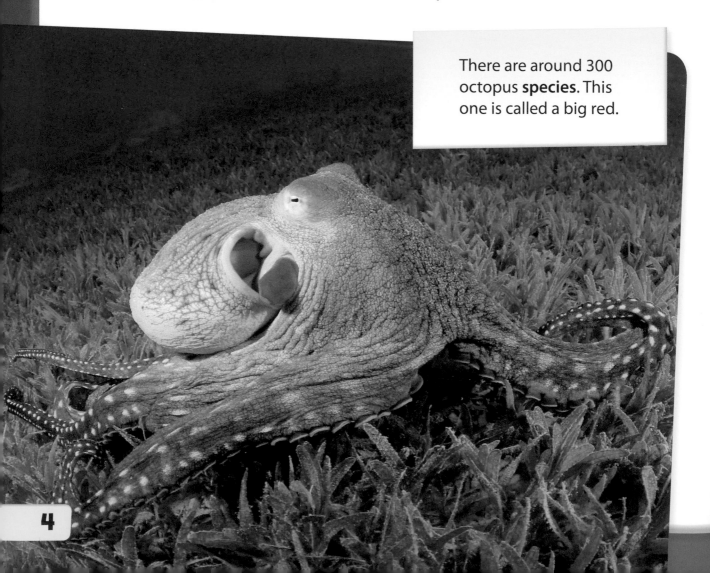

There are around 300 octopus **species**. This one is called a big red.

Squishy but smart

Octopuses are **invertebrates**, which means they do not have a backbone. They have no skeletons at all, just a soft, squishy body. They are part of a group of animals called **molluscs**, and are related to slugs, snails, and clams.

Invertebrates often seem like pretty simple creatures. But octopuses (along with their close relatives, squid and cuttlefish) have some amazing skills and abilities, and behave in all kinds of clever and cunning ways.

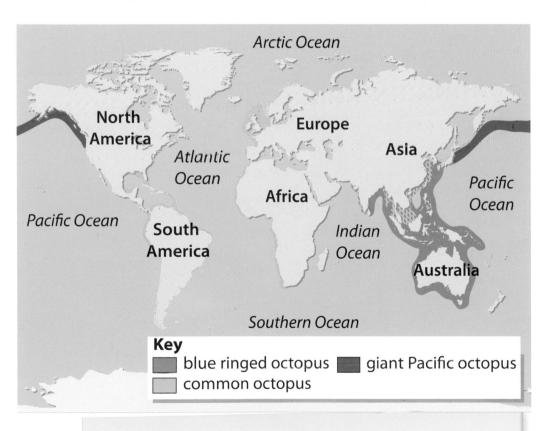

Octopuses live almost everywhere in the oceans, from rock pools and reefs, to the deep seabed. This map shows where some of the octopuses you will find out about in this book live.

Being an octopus

Many octopuses are **nocturnal**. They rest during the day and come out at night to hunt **prey** such as crabs and clams. Octopuses can crawl along on the seabed using their arms, or swim along in the water.

Living alone

Most octopuses live alone. They like feeling enclosed, so they make a cosy den in a pile of rocks, in a gap in coral, or even in an old oil barrel. They rest and eat their food in the den.

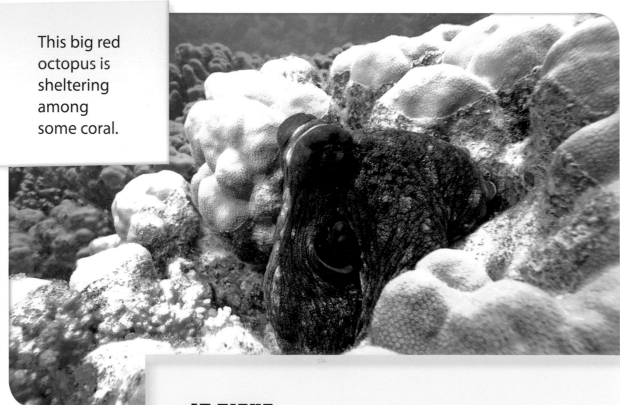

This big red octopus is sheltering among some coral.

AT RISK?

No octopuses have been listed as **endangered**, because not enough is known about them yet. However, experts think some types could be at risk of dying out.

Octopus sizes

The common octopus has a body as big as a football, with arms up to 1 metre (3 feet) long. Other octopuses range from small enough to sit in your hand, to ocean giants with arms 4 metres (13 feet) long.

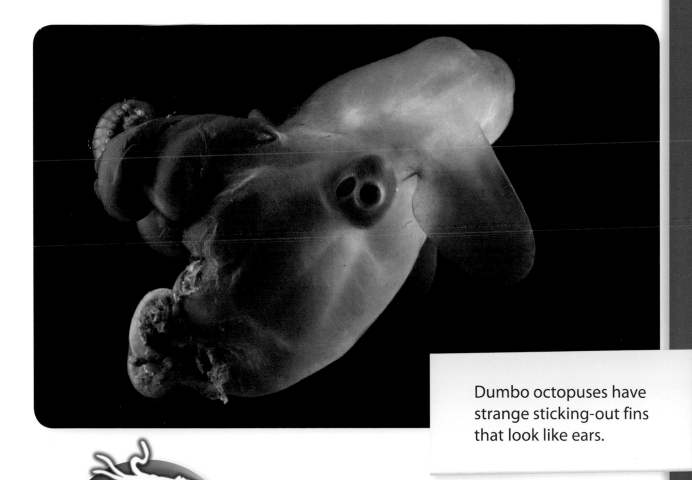

Dumbo octopuses have strange sticking-out fins that look like ears.

HOW DO WE KNOW?

As humans can't breathe under water, studying sea creatures can be tricky. Scientists go diving or snorkelling to watch octopuses in the wild. They also study **captive** octopuses in aquariums and science labs.

Octopus bodies

In cartoons, octopuses are often shown with a large, oval head on top of their eight arms. In fact, this is the octopus's sack-shaped body, or mantle. Its head is between its body and its arms, with the hard mouth, or **beak**, in the middle. As octopuses have no bones or joints, the eight arms are packed with muscles that can make them curl, twist, and turn in all directions.

OCTOPUS INK

When in danger, an octopus can squirt black, gloopy ink out of its siphon to confuse attackers.

Octopus ink creates a confusing cloud in the water. It distracts the attacker while the octopus escapes.

Body bits

In this picture you can see all the most important bits of an octopus's body.

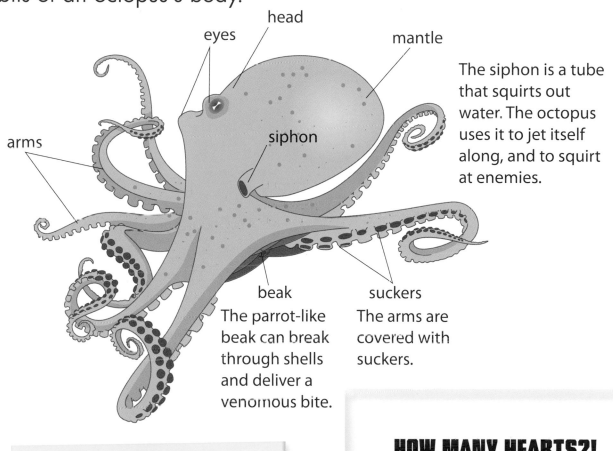

eyes

head

mantle

The siphon is a tube that squirts out water. The octopus uses it to jet itself along, and to squirt at enemies.

arms

siphon

beak

The parrot-like beak can break through shells and deliver a venomous bite.

suckers

The arms are covered with suckers.

Suckers help the octopus to grip onto its prey.

HOW MANY HEARTS?!

Octopuses have three hearts, and their blood is blue!

Octopus brains and senses

Scientists have found that octopuses actually have nine brains! Besides the main brain in the head, each octopus arm has its own "mini-brain". These mini-brains are long bundles of nerves that deal with all the arms' movements and sensations, as this would be too much for a single brain to manage.

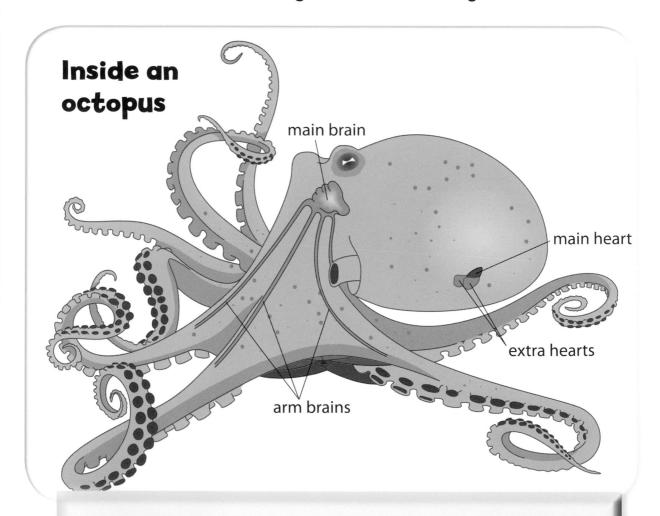

Inside an octopus

main brain

main heart

extra hearts

arm brains

BIG BRAINS

Octopuses have large brains for their body size, which could partly explain why they are so clever. Other animals that have big brains for their body size include tree shrews, humans, chimpanzees, dolphins, and crows.

Super-sensors

Octopus arms and suckers are amazingly sensitive. An octopus feels around with them, poking into narrow cracks in search of prey. Besides their brilliant sense of touch, the suckers can taste and smell, too. Octopuses use them to check whether what they are touching is good to eat, and to sense smells and tastes floating in the water.

Octopuses also have very good eyesight. They have no ears, but can hear a little by using other body parts to sense the ripples made by sounds.

Octopuses have large eyes with slit-shaped pupils.

In disguise

Octopuses are masters of **camouflage** and disguise. Chameleons are famous for changing colour, but an octopus can do it much better and much faster. Even more amazing, octopuses can also change their shape and texture.

For example, an octopus can make itself look just like a clump of frilly seaweed or a knobbly rock, then transform back into a smooth, rounded octopus shape again. Or it can flash a series of bright colours across its skin.

This common octopus is cleverly matching its body to the surrounding rocks and seaweed.

The mimic octopus can disguise itself as other animals. This one is pretending to be a dangerous sea snake.

How do they do it?

Camouflage tricks help octopuses to confuse and startle **predators**, hide for safety, or sneak up on their prey.

An octopus's skin is covered in tiny colour spots called chromatophores, surrounded by muscles. The muscles control each spot to make it much bigger, or make it disappear. This lets an octopus create all kinds of different patterns on its skin. It can also tighten muscles under its skin to change its shape and create a bumpy or knobbly surface texture.

A TIGHT SQUEEZE!

An octopus can make its squishy body so narrow that it can squeeze through a hole almost as small as its own eyeball.

Learning

Some animal abilities, such as the way a spider spins a web, are instincts. This means they are built into an animal's brain and happen automatically. But most animals can learn things, too.

Experiments have shown that octopuses are great learners. They can learn to recognize different shapes, or get a snack out of a maze. They can even learn to do a task, such as opening a box, by copying another octopus.

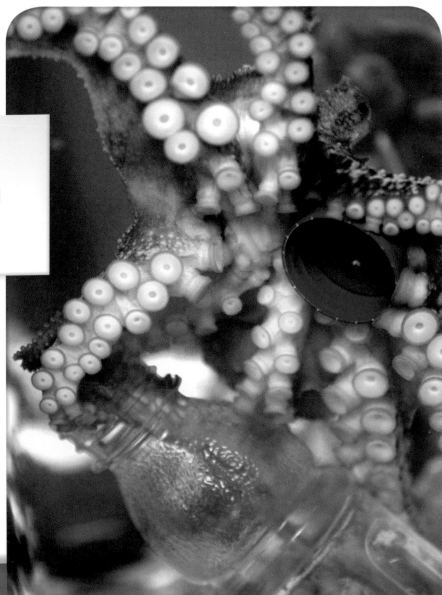

This captive octopus named Octi has unscrewed a plastic bottle to reach a snack.

How and why?

Most clever animals, such as humans, chimps, and dolphins, live in groups, and learn from their families as they grow up. Octopuses are different. Most species only live for a year or two. Also, octopus parents die when their eggs hatch, and don't teach their babies anything. So why are they so good at learning? Scientists still aren't sure.

After they hatch, baby octopuses must fend for themselves.

HOW DO WE KNOW?

An Italian scientist called Graziano Fiorito is famous for his octopus experiments. In one test, an octopus managed to open a screw-top jar after seeing another octopus do it first. It seemed to learn the trick just by watching.

Solving problems

When faced with a problem, octopuses will keep trying to work it out. They can find their way through mazes, work out how to reach a hidden treat, or search for an escape route from a tank. And if they succeed, they'll remember the solution for next time.

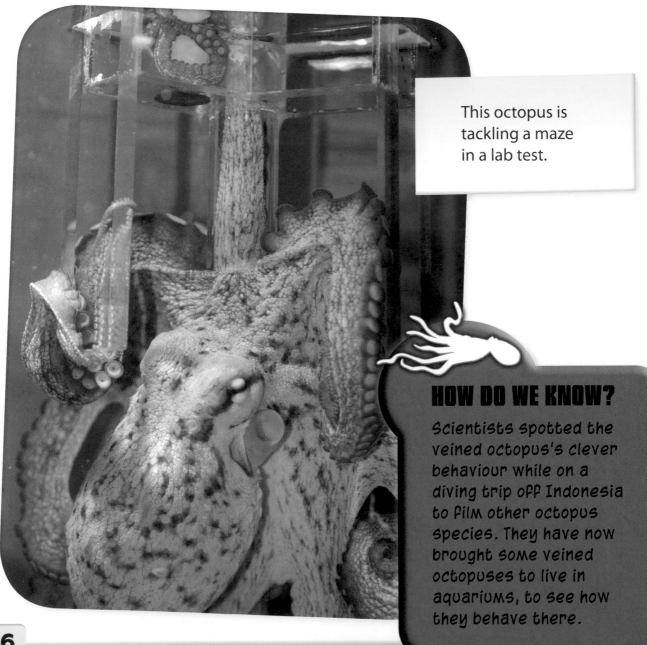

This octopus is tackling a maze in a lab test.

HOW DO WE KNOW?

Scientists spotted the veined octopus's clever behaviour while on a diving trip off Indonesia to film other octopus species. They have now brought some veined octopuses to live in aquariums, to see how they behave there.

A better way

Like other intelligent animals, octopuses often find new ways of doing things. In the wild, they collect stones or shells to make doors for their dens. Some use their siphons as cleaning jets to blow their food leftovers, such as broken seashells, out of their dens.

The veined octopus of south-east Asia carries seashells or coconut shells around with it, and uses them to hide inside. To do this, the octopus must be smart enough to plan ahead, and think about what things could be used for. Scientists think the veined octopus is one of the few invertebrates known to use tools.

A veined octopus walks on tiptoe, carrying useful shells under its body.

Sneaky tricks

A famous octopus story dates from the 1870s, when staff at an aquarium in Brighton were puzzled to find fish were going missing. One morning, an octopus was found in with the fish. It had been sneaking out of its own tank in the night, stealing fish to eat, then going home again!

Octopuses can survive for a while in the open air. This is why they sometimes go exploring out of their tanks.

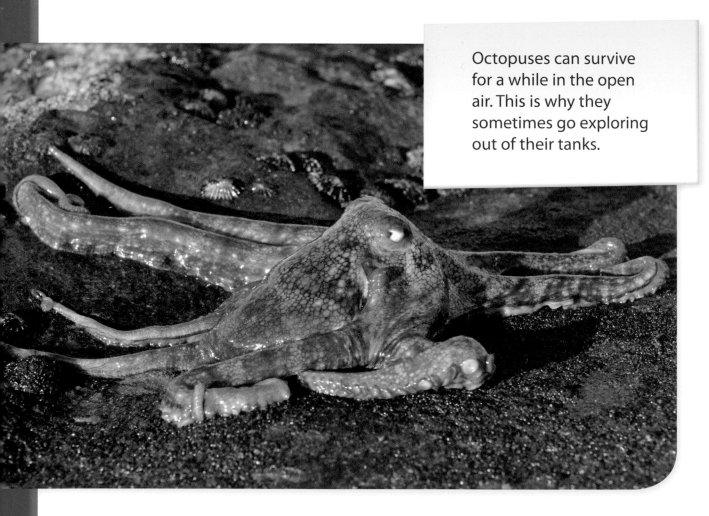

Octopuses are great escape artists. Scientists and aquarium staff often find them on the floor, hiding in drains or even crawling up shelves. They are strong and can push up tank lids and pull out plugs, as well as wriggling through tiny cracks.

Out of the water!

Octopuses breathe under water, but as long as their bodies are wet, they can survive in the air for a while. In the wild, they sometimes scramble over rocks and seaweed between rock pools. They can also escape from fish markets and try to slither away on the pavement.

ARMLESS OCTOPUS

The banded drop-arm octopus can shed an arm deliberately as a way to avoid being eaten. The arm wriggles around to distract the predator while the octopus escapes. The octopus can then regrow the arm. This regrowing is called regeneration.

This octopus has lost two of its arms, but they are growing back again.

Having fun

Do octopuses play? It can be hard to tell, but some do appear to enjoy themselves!

Playing alone

Many animals like playing together. As octopuses live alone in the wild, they don't do this. However, it's possible to play on your own, and some experts believe many octopuses really do like playing with toys.

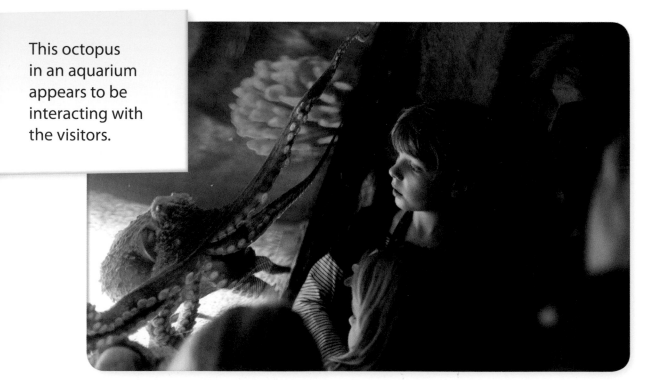

This octopus in an aquarium appears to be interacting with the visitors.

PET OCTOPUSES

Keeping a pet octopus might sound like fun, but it's not a good idea unless you're an expert. Octopuses need special salt water and lots of cleaning and feeding — and they don't live for very long.

HOW DO WE KNOW?

In one test, scientists gave captive octopuses empty pill bottles. They all handled the bottles for a while, but two played games with them. One kept blowing hers into the water current, then waiting for it to "bounce" back like a ball.

Look at me!

In aquariums, octopuses sometimes seem to dance around and get excited when visitors are there. They may follow people to and fro or even show off a series of shape and colour changes. Keepers and owners also say octopuses can recognize people they know.

Staff may give toys to octopuses in aquariums so they can use the skills they would use in the wild. This may stop them from getting bored.

Humans and octopuses

Humans have a long history with octopuses. For centuries, we mainly just wanted to catch them and eat them! In the past, we used octopus ink for writing. More recently, we've begun to keep octopuses in aquariums and as pets. Scientists have been able to learn much more about them.

Old legends tell of octopus-like sea monsters dragging down ships. However, no known octopus is big enough to do this.

These octopuses are for sale at a fish market in Japan.

What does an octopus taste like?

People usually describe octopus meat as smooth, chewy, and slightly fishy-tasting. It's quite a healthy food, and is very popular in Italy, Spain, Portugal, Japan, and Korea. However, some people think it's not right to eat such an intelligent animal.

PAUL, THE WORLD CUP OCTOPUS

In 2010, a common octopus living at a Sea Life Centre in Germany predicted the winners of eight World Cup football matches in a row, including the final. He picked his favourites by choosing from two food boxes marked with the playing teams' national flags. No one knows how he decided!

Octopus science

To do experiments on octopuses, scientists usually catch them from the wild. They also design their experiments carefully, to suit octopus abilities.

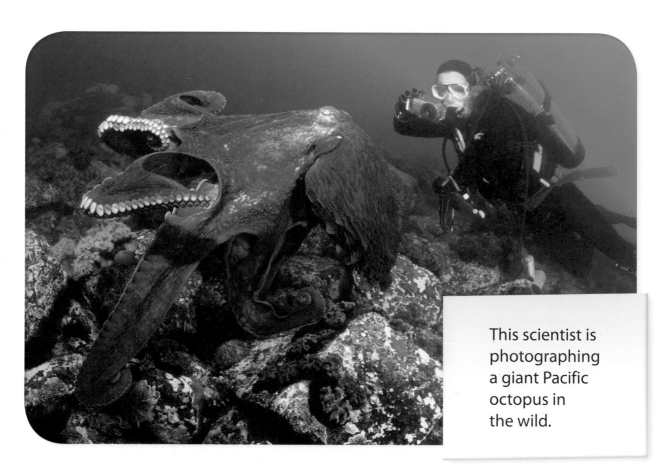

This scientist is photographing a giant Pacific octopus in the wild.

Getting it right

In experiments with octopuses, mazes, puzzles, and toys have to work well under water. Octopuses must be kept in separate tanks, or they might eat each other. If a maze leads to a tasty crab or mussel reward, all the equipment must be clean, with no fishy scent trails. Otherwise, the octopus might simply be following the smell rather than working out the maze.

Personality test

In the 1990s, scientists tested 44 red octopuses to see if they had different personalities. They wrote down how each octopus behaved when it was approached, touched with a brush, and fed, over a two-week period. Some octopuses were much bolder, more active, or touchier, while others were more relaxed or shy.

OCTOPUS CHEMICALS

Besides octopus behaviour, scientists study octopuses' muscles and brains, and the chemicals in their bodies. Studies of octopus bite **venom** have found they contain chemicals that could make medicines for treating allergies or cancer.

This giant Pacific octopus is being tagged so that scientists can track its movements at sea.

Copying the octopus

Octopuses and their amazing abilities have inspired some super-cool inventions, both old and new.

Sticky suckers

Have you noticed rubber or plastic suction cups on bath mats, toys, and other objects? They were developed in the 1860s, and were based on the shape of octopus suckers. Large suction cups are used to carry sheets of glass, and people have even used specially designed rubber suckers to climb skyscrapers!

PART OCTOPUS

One inventor has designed a wriggly **prosthetic** octopus arm that can be attached to a human arm. It shows how this type of robot could help people who have lost limbs.

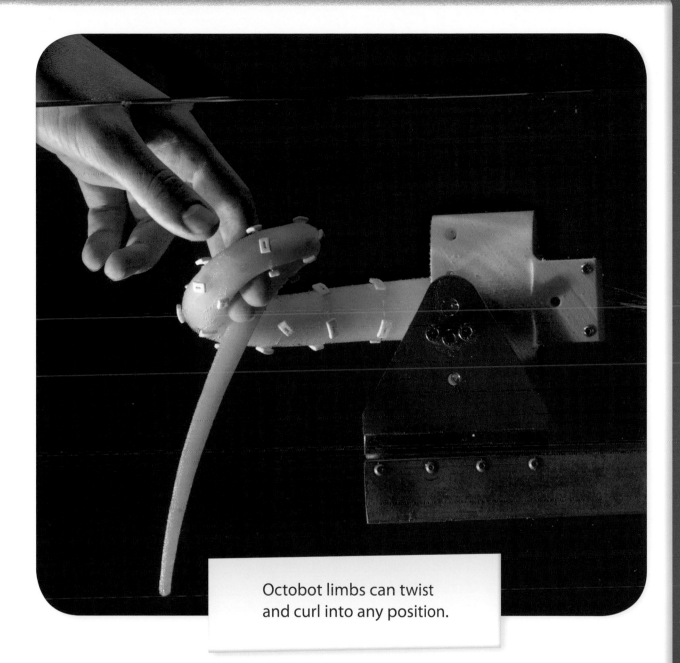

Octobot limbs can twist
and curl into any position.

Octobots!

Some scientists are making a new type of robot that
copies the way octopuses move their arms. Most
robots have hard, fixed limbs that work like our
bones and muscles. "Octobot" limbs are bendy.
In the future, octobots could be used to carry out
underwater rescues.

The amazing octopus

There are a lot of amazing animals out there, but octopuses really are extraordinary. Their shape-shifting and colour-changing abilities, disappearing acts, and clever tricks make them seem almost alien. Yet these are creatures we used to think were pretty simple – boneless, blob-like, and tasty in a stew. As scientists keep studying octopuses, imagine what else they could discover!

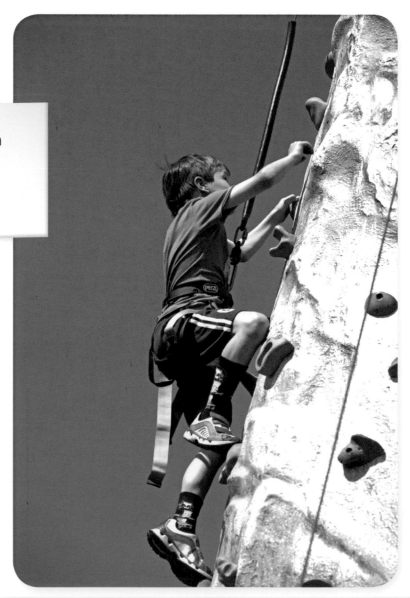

Climbing is much harder work for us than it is for an octopus.

Octopus superpowers

As you're human, you're already intelligent and good at learning and problem-solving. But what if you could have any of the octopus's amazing abilities?

- If you had eight arms covered with suckers, they would be useful for multitasking, and your super sucker grip would be great for sport and climbing.

- If you had shape-shifting abilities, you could squeeze through tiny gaps, create all sorts of crazy costumes, or turn your body into an umbrella on a rainy day.

- If you had colour-changing skills, you could blend into the background so that no one could see you!

- If you had a water siphon for jetting along, you'd zoom through the pool and break every swimming record.

- If you had squirty ink, you could splat anyone who bothered you, and maybe invent a new way of painting, too!

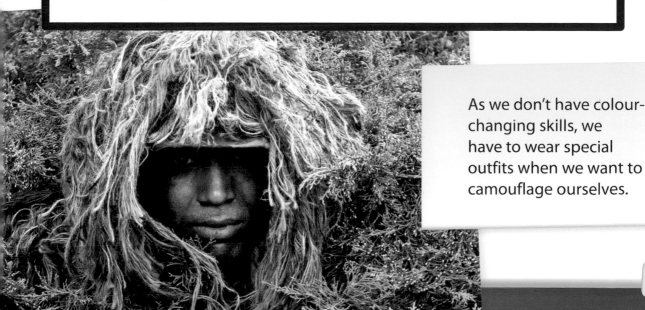

As we don't have colour-changing skills, we have to wear special outfits when we want to camouflage ourselves.

Glossary

beak an octopus's hard, biting mouth, shaped a bit like a parrot's beak

camouflage colours and patterns that blend in with the background or surroundings

captive held in a zoo, aquarium, or laboratory instead of living in the wild

endangered at risk of dying out

invertebrate animal without a backbone

mollusc animal without a backbone, with a soft body and a shell; part of the group that includes slugs, snails, and mussels

nocturnal active at night

predator animal that hunts and eats other animals

prey animal that is eaten by other animals

prosthetic human-made body part, made to replace a part that is missing

species particular type of living thing

squid type of animal related to the octopus. Squid have a long head rather than a rounded one, and eight arms and two tentacles.

tentacle long, thin body part, often with a paddle-shaped section at the end, found in squid, but not octopuses

venom poison from a bite or sting

Find out more

Books

Gentle Giant Octopus (Nature Storybooks), Karen Wallace (Walker Books, 2012)

Octopus (A Day in the Life: Sea Animals), Louise Spilsbury (Raintree, 2011)

Websites

www.arkive.org/common-octopus/octopus-vulgaris
A selection of amazing octopus photos and videos, as well as fascinating facts and links, can be found on the Arkive website.

www.bbc.co.uk/nature/life/Octopus
The BBC Nature website includes links to amazing giant octopus and dumbo octopus videos.

www.nhm.ac.uk/kids-only/life/life-sea/index.html
Learn more about life in the sea on the Natural History Museum's website.

Places to visit

There are lots of aquariums around the world where you can come face to face with real live octopuses. Those listed below keep octopuses, but always check before you go, as octopuses do not live for long and are not always on show.

Blue Planet Aquarium
Cheshire Oaks, Cheshire CH65 9LF
www.blueplanetaquarium.com

Sea Life Loch Lomond
Loch Lomond Shores, Balloch G83 8QL
www.visitsealife.com/Loch-lomond

Index

arms 4, 6, 7, 8, 9, 10, 11, 29
arms, shedding 19

babies 15
beaks 8, 9, 30
big red octopuses 4, 6
blood 9
blue ringed octopuses 5
body parts 9
brains 10, 14, 25
breathing 19

camouflage 12–13, 29, 30
captive octopuses 7, 14, 16, 18,
   20–21, 22, 30
chromatophores 13
common octopuses 5, 7, 12, 23

dens 6, 17
dumbo octopuses 7

endangered species 6, 30
escaping 18, 19
eyes 9, 11
eyesight 11

giant Pacific octopuses 5, 24, 25

habitats 5
hearing 11
hearts 9, 10

ink 8, 22, 29
instincts 14
intelligence 10, 16–17
invertebrates 5, 17, 30

learning 14–15
legends 22
lifespan 15

mantle 8, 9
maze tests 16, 24
medicines 25
mimic octopuses 13
molluscs 5, 30

narrow gaps, squeezing through 13
nocturnal creatures 6, 30

octobot limbs 27
octopus meat 23

Paul (World Cup octopus) 23
personalities 25
playing 20–21
predators 13, 19, 30
prey 6, 9, 11, 13, 30
prosthetic arms 26, 30

red octopuses 25
regeneration 19
robots 26, 27

senses 11
siphons 8, 9, 17, 29
size 7
skin 13
species 4, 30
squid 4, 30
studying octopuses 7, 24–25
suckers 9, 11, 26, 29
suction cups 26

tentacles 4, 30
tools, using 17

veined octopuses 16, 17
venom 25, 30